GW01605614

My Wonderful Gift Book of

Fairy Tales

PRINTED IN GREAT BRITAIN
DEAN & SON Ltd.
52 54 Southwark St. LONDON SE1 1UA
TRADE MARK

0 603 00164

CONTENTS

ALI BABA AND THE FORTY THIEVES	6
SNOW WHITE AND THE SEVEN DWARFS	32
SINBAD THE SAILOR	58
RUMPELSTILTSKIN	84
CINDERELLA	110

The stories and illustrations in this edition previously published by Dean as separate titles.

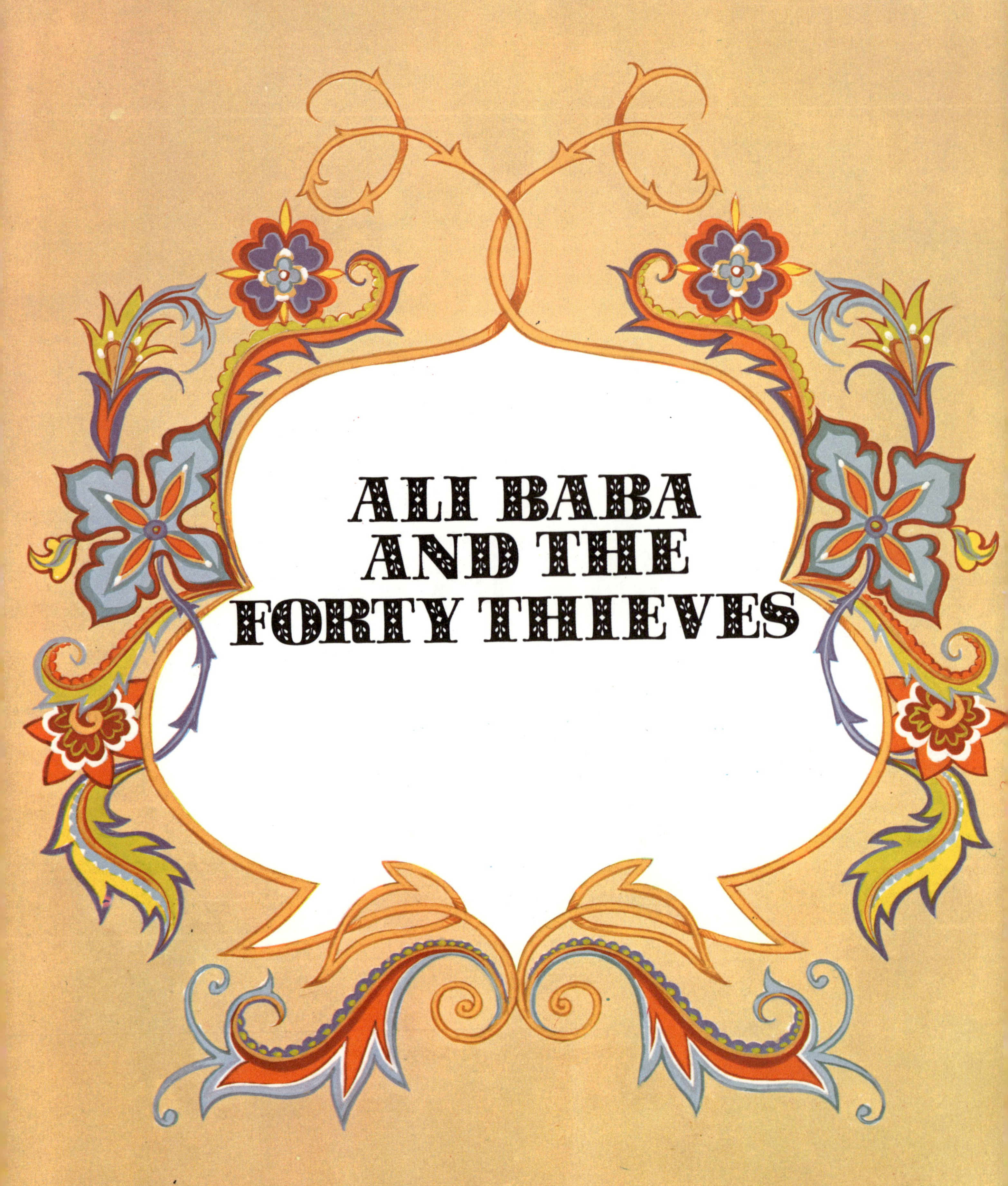

ALI BABA AND THE FORTY THIEVES

There were once two brothers living in the land of Persia. The older one, Cassim, had married a wealthy woman and become a man of substance. Ali Baba, the younger one, had married a girl as poor as himself and became a humble woodcutter. Cassim dwelt in a large house, employed many servants and looked down his nose at Ali Baba, whose house was very tiny and had a leaky roof. Ali Baba was quite resigned to the fact that he would never be a rich man, just as his brother devoutly hoped that he would never become a poor one.

Life often has surprises in store when one least expects them, and so it was that Ali Baba, while chopping wood in the forest, was quite unprepared for what was about to happen.

As he worked, Ali Baba hummed a tune to himself. Soon he found that he had to hum very loudly because there was a lot of noise going on. He stopped humming to try to identify the sound. It was the pounding of hooves and they were approaching the spot where Ali Baba stood. Being a cautious man, Ali Baba made himself scarce. He hid behind a large rock and peered out to see who was coming.

A band of horsemen was riding towards him. Their leader was a tall dark man. When the riders were close enough for Ali Baba to see their faces, he saw that this man looked ruthless and frightening. The riders were nearing some rocks. From his place of concealment Ali Baba saw them rein their horses and the leader rise up in his saddle. He pointed at the rock and in a commanding voice shouted: "OPEN SESAME!"

What followed now was almost too incredible for Ali Baba to believe, even though he saw it with his own eyes. There was a great rumbling and trembling, and slowly an opening appeared where previously there had been none. The horsemen rode in and the cave closed up. There was no sign of any door. Ali Baba was too terrified to move. He stood trembling and waited to see what would happen next. Quite soon he heard the same sound as before and saw the horsemen emerge through the opening which again, as if by magic, had appeared. This time Ali Baba counted the men. There were forty of them. As they issued from the cave he saw that their saddle bags were now empty. "They must be robbers hiding their treasure," thought Ali Baba and hid further behind his rock. "They will surely cut my throat if they realise that I have discovered their hiding place."

When the robbers had gone, Ali Baba crept out from his place of concealment and began to run home. As he

ran he thought about what he had witnessed. He slowed down, then he stopped. "I wonder," he thought, "what would happen if I tried to get into the cave. Probably it would not open for me at all, but if it did . . ." Quickly he turned back the way he had come and stopped at the spot where he had seen the robber chief rein his horse. He took a deep breath: "OPEN SESAME!" he roared at the top of his voice. Nothing happened. Ali Baba sadly turned away. "Oh well," he said. Just then there was a great crescendo of sound as the cave opened. Ali Baba laughed with delight and hurried in. The great door in the rock shut behind him, and Ali Baba was confronted by a sight such as his eyes had never seen before.

The whole cave blazed with shimmering light. The floor

was strewn with exotic treasure. Precious stones lay in heaps among goblets of gold and vases of crystal. Sacks overflowed with necklaces and rings of the finest workmanship. Ali Baba stood for a moment as if turned to stone and gasped at the dazzling sight. Then he began to fill his pockets with as much treasure as they would hold. He was very careful to take only one thing from each pile so that the robbers would not suspect that someone had found their hoard.

Soon he could carry no more, and without delay he returned to the spot where the door had been. Again Ali Baba spoke the words of power: "OPEN SESAME!" This time, without any delay, he was able to walk out of the fantastic cave.

This time he did hurry home to his wife. At first she did not believe her husband and scolded him for getting drunk and imagining things, but when he showed her the jewels concealed in his pockets she realised that he must be speaking the truth.

After supper Ali Baba and his wife sat down to count their money and jewels. Neither of them had possessed anything much worth counting in the past, so they were not very good at it. Finally Ali Baba's wife gave up. "I know what I shall do," she said. "I will borrow a measuring cup from your brother Cassim's wife and we can see how much treasure we have without all this trouble."

Off she went without delay. The wife of Cassim knew that Ali Baba was penniless and wondered what her sister-in-law could possibly want with a measuring cup. Being of an inquisitive disposition, she determined to find out. "Of course you may borrow my measuring cup," she said. "I will just fetch it from my husband's storeroom for you."

Before she gave the cup to Ali Baba's wife she decided to put a small patch of thick glue at the bottom of the vessel. Anything that was measured in the cup would then stick to this and the secret would be out.

Ali Baba's wife accepted the cup gratefully and, not suspecting anything, took it home. Immediately, Ali Baba began to fill it from the small pile of jewels which lay in front of him on the floor. It was much easier to count them by the cupful and the work was soon completed. Ali Baba sent his wife to return the cup. Neither of them had any idea

that inside it, stuck to the glue, was a bright, shiny gold coin.

When Cassim's wife saw the coin in the cup she hurried to her husband and began to nag him: "Cassim, you must go straight to the house of that awful brother of yours and find out where this money has come from. Why, he never possessed two pennies to rub together." Cassim looked at the coin she held in her hand. He had never seen gold of such high quality. Surely, if his brother had a secret source of wealth, it was only right that he should share it with his nearest relative.

It was too late to do anything about it that night, but Cassim determined that early next morning he would discover from Ali Baba the source of his wealth.

As soon as he awoke the next day Cassim set off to his brother's house. It was so early that Ali Baba was still asleep, but his wife invited Cassim in to wait while she woke her husband. Cassim sat in the tiny kitchen and looked around him. He noticed that above the fireplace some of the bricks appeared to be coming loose. He decided to take a closer look. He put his hand on the edge of one of the bricks to push it into place, but it fell right out as he touched it. In the cavity behind it Cassim was astonished to see something glittering. Unable to restrain his curiosity, he slipped in his hand to feel what it was, and pulled out a handful of beautiful gems. Cassim could hardly believe his own eyes.

He was just about to slip his hand into the hole in the wall again when Ali Baba entered the room. Cassim felt rather embarrassed at being caught prying so he began to shout: "What kind of a brother do you think you are, keeping secrets from one who loves you so dearly as I? I suppose that you had no intention of sharing your good fortune with anyone as humble as myself. Probably I am not good enough for you now that you are so rich."

Ali Baba was quite amazed at his brother's outburst. He began to feel that perhaps he had treated his brother unfairly by not telling him. He decided to remedy this straight away, just as Cassim thought that he would.

Cassim was very eager to hear all that Ali Baba had to say. As soon as he heard about the hoard of treasure he felt that nothing would suffice but that he should increase his own wealth by depriving the robbers of some of theirs.

"They are only thieves," he said to Ali Baba. "Just as they have deprived innocent folk, so I shall deprive them."

He hurried home to prepare his pack of mules, and as soon as they were made ready with large baskets to contain the treasure, he set off along the road Ali Baba had described.

It did not take Cassim long to reach the spot at which the cave opened. He took a piece of parchment out of his pocket and in a brave voice read out the words upon it: "OPEN SESAME!"

At once the cave entrance appeared with a great rumbling. Cassim threw away the parchment and strode in, leading his pack of animals. He did not stop to admire the magnificence spread before him. Greedily and swiftly he filled the panniers which the mules had on their backs. Suddenly Cassim heard the sound of movement outside the cave. He realised that the robbers must be about to enter. As fast as he could, he led the animals further into the cave in search of concealment.

"Open Sesame!" roared the robber chief. He and his men rode into the cave, dismounted and tethered their horses. They began to unload the baskets they carried. One of the men gave a shout: "Mahmoud, someone has been here! I am sure that there was more in that sack than there is now. I should know, as I brought it myself." All the thieves gathered round the speaker and waited to hear what their chief would say. After looking around, Mahmoud spoke softly: "Quietly, men. Let us search every corner of the cave."

"The villain may still be concealed here. The man who finds him may have the pleasure of slitting his throat."

The men dispersed and in no time at all Cassim was found. Before he could even beg for mercy he was dead and his head was cut off. The robbers thought it was a fair revenge for his crime, stealing from them. They left his body where it lay and went on their way.

By that evening Cassim's wife was beginning to be worried about her husband. Never had he stayed away from home for so long. She begged Ali Baba to go and find out what had become of him. Ali Baba did not really want to return to the cave, but he felt obliged to help his sister-in-law.

What a sight met his eyes when he entered the cave! There lay the dead body of his brother Cassim. With a heavy heart, Ali Baba turned homewards. He did not know how he was going to break the news to his sister-in-law about the death of her husband. His brother's body Ali Baba had put into a sack which the donkey he had been riding now carried. At least his brother would be buried properly and not be left in the cave.

Ali Baba had a friend in the house of Cassim; it was Morgiana, the serving maid. She was betrothed to the son of Ali Baba, but they were as yet too poor to wed. It was to this girl that Ali Baba related the terrible story of his brother's death. He asked her to convey the bad news to her mistress and remind her to keep silent about where Cassim had been when he met his untimely end.

Morgiana was an intelligent girl and realised immediately what it would mean if the thieves ever discovered that someone else knew of the whereabouts of their treasure cache. She suggested to Ali Baba that Cassim should be buried just as if he had died at home in his own bed. She knew of a craftsman who lived not too far away and was very good at sewing leather garments. She would ask him to sew a coat with a tight hood into which the body of Cassim and his head could be fitted.

The next day Cassim was buried. His wife informed the friends of her husband that he had just passed away in his sleep. The ruse was so successful that no one suspected Cassim's wife of lying.

That might have been the end of that if Mahmoud and his band of robbers had not been back to their hideout, but of course they had soon collected enough treasure to make the trip to the cave necessary. On entering, they were most surprised to see that the body of Cassim was no longer there. "Someone else knows our secret," shouted Mahmoud. "We must discover without delay who it is. I personally shall cut off the culprit's head!"

He led his men out of the cave and sent them into the town to mingle with the people and try to discover something useful.

It was Mahmoud himself who chanced to meet the man who had made the coat for Cassim to be buried in. "What goes on in this great town of yours?" Mahmoud inquired. "I am not the one to ask," replied the man. "I am far too busy working to notice anything. Why, only last week I was expected to sew a fine coat for a man to be buried in, and I only had one evening to do the job in. Everyone is in such a hurry nowadays."

Mahmoud was very interested in the coat the man had made. He invited him into the inn for a drink of tea and to hear more about it. The man was quite willing to talk, and before long Mahmoud had gathered all the information that he required. Apparently the man had been blindfolded and taken to a house where a body was laid out for him to measure for the coat. "I think that the poor devil must have broken his neck," said the fellow. "It did not seem to be in the right position at all, but no matter, I was paid for the job. They gave me five gold pieces."

"I will double that if you can take me to that house," said Mahmoud, who was now sure that the man could be speaking only of the body of Cassim. The coatmaker at first protested that he would be unable to find the house again. The robber chief suggested that if he were blindfolded again it might prove easier. To this the man finally consented.

The man led Mahmoud straight to the house of Ali Baba. On receipt of his ten coins he hurried off. Mahmoud stayed behind just long enough to make a chalk mark upon the door. "I shall be back later with my men," he thought.

Luckily for Ali Baba, not long after the mark was made, Morgiana noticed it on her way to the market. She guessed that somehow the thieves had discovered their whereabouts. She hurried into the house for a piece of chalk and then proceeded to mark all the doors in the street in the same way in which Ali Baba's door had been marked.

Later that night, in a murderous mood, Mahmoud and his men returned to kill the one who was possessed of their secret. How surprised and angered they were to discover that all the houses in the street were marked with the same sign.

Next morning the coatmaker was again persuaded, for five more gold coins, to point out the house to which he had been led. Once again he did so, and Mahmoud made a different mark upon the door, but, as luck would have it, Morgiana was again able to help Ali Baba by marking the other doors in the street.

For the second time the robbers were outwitted, and for the last time the coatmaker pointed out the house. This time Mahmoud did not rely on chalk marks. Instead he committed to memory as many details about the house as he was able, to remember it again.

Several days later the robber chief disguised himself as a seller of oil. He prepared thirty-nine huge clay jars which could be attached to either side of a camel's harness. He ordered his men to climb into the jars and not emerge until ordered to do so.

Ali Baba was a very hospitable man. When he heard from the oil merchant about how far he had travelled that day, he invited him to stay and share a meal. The merchant was most happy to do so. Morgiana was sent out to feed the merchant's animals.

She was amazed at the sight of so many jars of oil and wondered if she ought to summon a stable boy to feed the camels. She wondered also if the jars were full or empty. She decided to look into one. As she began to raise the lid a voice spoke from inside the jar: "Is it time yet?"

Morgiana was terrified but managed to stammer, "Not yet!" in as gruff a voice as she could muster.

It was clear to Morgiana that the oil seller must be no other than the robber chief. She was equally convinced that the jars contained not oil but thieves. Without delay she hurried into the kitchen and set a great copper pot on to boil. Time and time again she filled kettles with the steaming water and carried them out into the courtyard. One by one she filled the jars with boiling water until all the thirty-nine thieves were dead.

In the morning the oil merchant departed without Morgiana being able to talk to Ali Baba about who his guest was. When he eventually did find out, he was more than grateful to her for her quick thinking. He wanted to give her a reward, a dowry composed of precious stones and gold. Morgiana was very grateful and said that she would be very happy to take the reward and settle down as the wife of Ali Baba's son, but not yet. The robber chief would be sure to return, and this time his revenge would be much worse than before.

The words of Morgiana were shortly proved right, for quite soon a new shop opened in the street where Ali Baba lived. The shopkeeper did not in any way resemble the oil

merchant but Morgiana recognised him by the ring he wore. She decided to keep a close watch on the man in case he came to harm the father of her betrothed.

Ali Baba was not a suspicious man and soon made friends with the new shopkeeper. He even invited him to dinner. Morgiana watched Mahmoud throughout the meal, and once, as he turned to look at something that Ali Baba pointed out to him, she caught a glimpse of a dagger in his belt.

"I would dearly love to dance for our guest," she said, and before Ali Baba could protest she was on her feet swirling and turning gracefully and laughing aloud. As she spun round and round she came nearer and nearer to the guest. Suddenly she turned and plunged a dagger into his chest. Ali Baba was aghast. A guest had been murdered in his own home by the very girl that was to marry his son. He ordered servants to bind her and lead her from the room. Morgiana did not protest, but Ali Baba's son, seeing that his beloved was being unfairly judged, leapt up and confronted his father, "Oh, Father," he cried, "do you not realise who this man is? He would have slain you if it were not for the quick thinking of Morgiana."

Ali Baba was eventually convinced that his son spoke the truth. He begged Morgiana to forgive him for his unfair judgment of her. "Now you must wed my son," he cried, "and become my own true daughter." Morgiana, of course, agreed.

Soon Ali Baba and his wife were able to be present at the wedding of their son to the faithful Morgiana. For a wedding present from Ali Baba they received two words, "OPEN SESAME", and the instructions on how to reach the treasure cave.

This secret was to be theirs alone until they were able to pass it on to their children.

SNOW WHITE
AND THE
SEVEN DWARFS

Long ago, in a distant land of dark forests and high, snow-capped mountains, there was a beautiful castle. It was surrounded by lovely gardens where sweet-scented roses grew amongst beds of brightly coloured flowers and shrubs. Shady trees protected these colourful gardens from the hot sun in the summer and the cold winds in winter. There were great lawns, and ornamental pools in which gold and silver fish darted between the shimmering water-lilies.

There was one thing missing in the gardens and that was the sound of children's laughter, and this was a great disappointment to the young King and Queen who lived in the castle. They were very much in love, but also very unhappy, for they had no sons or daughters of their own.

One springtime, when the flowers were in bud, and the trees were covered in blossom, the Queen walked round the garden, sighing and looking sadly at the beauty around her. "I wish I had a daughter to share my lovely garden with," she thought.

The Queen's wish must have been heard, for on the day of the first snow a baby girl was born to her.

There should have been great rejoicing at this happy event, but alas, on the same day, the young Queen died.

The little girl was a beautiful baby. Her hair was a mass of jet black curls and her face and hands were as white as the snowflakes which fell outside the window of her nursery. Her cheeks were pink as apple blossom and her eyes as blue as the sky on a summer's day. No-one could but love her. The King decided to call his daughter Snow White.

The seasons passed in the garden. Spring was followed by summer, the leaves of the trees turned red, brown and gold in autumn, and all was white and sparkling in winter. The years came and went, and Snow White grew from a small child into a beautiful young girl. She tended the garden lovingly as her mother had done, and was loved by the birds and the other animals who lived there. She was a good daughter, and the King was sad because she did not have a mother. Eventually he decided to marry again. He had thought about this a great deal, and had met many ladies of royal blood who would make a suitable queen and mother.

His choice finally fell on a princess from a far-away country. No-one seemed to know anything of the place she came from—it was far beyond the mountains. He chose her because she was the most lovely and pleasant of all. The wedding took place amidst much rejoicing, and at last the King was happy. Snow White had a new mother.

Not long after, the King had to leave his castle to visit his cousin, the king of the neighbouring country, who was ill. He left happy in the sure knowledge that his new wife would take care of his dear Snow White.

If he had but noticed the gleam in his wife's green eyes as he bade her goodbye, he would never have gone, and this story would not have been written. But he did go, and from that day Snow White was in danger.

From her home beyond the mountains the new Queen had brought a large gold-framed mirror. This hung in her bed-chamber. But the mirror was no ordinary one, for it could speak. Each day, as the Queen combed her long hair, she would peer into it and ask:

"Mirror, mirror on the wall,
Who is fairest of them all?"

And each day the mirror would reply that of course the Queen was fairest. This would put her in a good temper for the rest of the morning.

One fateful day the mirror gave the wrong answer:

"Snow White is the fairest, that is true.
She is far lovelier than you."

The Queen was so enraged that she determined to get rid of Snow White for ever. She summoned one of her faithful servants, and told him to take Snow White into the depths of the forest and to return with only her heart, which he was to put into a small jewelled box.

The servant was not a cruel man. He did not want to kill Snow White, but he took her into the forest as the Queen had instructed him.

Once there, he told Snow White that she must never return to the castle. He left her in a small clearing and hurried away. On his way back to the castle he killed a deer and put the beast's heart into the Queen's jewelled box.

Left on her own, Snow White at first wandered happily around picking flowers and listening to the birds singing, but as the evening approached she began to get hungry and thirsty. She decided to look for a path to lead her out of the forest. This was not very easy to do. The trees cast deep shadows, and there were strange noises and rustlings all around her. She began to run.

Suddenly Snow White stopped. In front of her was a tiny gate and a path that led to the sweetest little cottage you could imagine. Snow White opened the gate and walked up to the door. No-one answered her knock, so she turned the handle. The door opened and Snow White walked in.

The inside of the cottage was very unusual, for there was only one room. There were no stairs at all. In the room stood a table with seven little chairs. Against the wall were seven little beds. There was also a large stove on which stood an array of pots and pans. The room looked rather dusty, and in the corners cobwebs hung from the ceiling.

As soon as Snow White caught sight of the beds, she wanted to go to sleep.

Of course the little beds were much too small, so she pushed them together and lay across them. She fell asleep almost immediately.

The little cottage belonged to seven little dwarfs, who worked in the nearby mountains mining precious stones and gold. As Snow White was falling asleep they were coming up the path to their home. The first dwarf opened the door and they all rushed in, stopping almost immediately in astonishment. Someone was asleep on their beds!

The bravest of the dwarfs moved forward a little to get a better look, and the others peeped out from behind him. "Oh," sighed the brave dwarf, "what a beautiful girl." The others pushed him out of the way so that they could also see. One of them bumped into a bed, and Snow White sat up in fright. "Who are you?" she cried. "I am sorry I came into your cottage."

The dwarfs quickly reassured her, and invited her to stay for as long as she wished. They even volunteered to sleep on the chairs so that she could have a comfortable night on their beds.

The next morning Snow White told them her story. The dwarfs were aghast at the wickedness of the Queen. "You must stay with us," they said. Snow White thanked them joyfully and promised to cook and keep house for them. She began straight away by dusting, and sweeping the floor.

The dwarfs went off to work happily, their minds full of their new guest.

Meanwhile, in the castle, the wicked Queen rewarded her servant for bringing Snow White's heart back from the forest. She held the box which contained the heart as she spoke to her magic mirror:

"Mirror, mirror on the wall,
Who is fairest of us all?"

The mirror replied without hesitation:

"In the forest far away
Dwells Snow White as fair as day.
Her beauty is without compare,
None in the land is half as fair."

The Queen's fury knew no bounds. She hurled the box against the wall and screamed with rage. She decided to kill Snow White herself.

She disguised herself as a gipsy woman with a basket of odds and ends to sell. Among them was a pretty, decorated comb. The comb was a special one. Before putting it into the basket the Queen dipped it in a very strong poison.

The Queen set off for the cottage. At the door she knocked and spoke in a disguised voice, "Pretty trinkets for sale, dearie. Buy a gift for your loved ones from a poor old gipsy."

Snow White had been told by the dwarfs not to open the door to strangers, so she unlatched the window and peered out. The old woman on the doorstep looked innocent enough, and the girl was curious to see what the basket contained. The old woman held the pretty comb out to her.

"See this?" she cackled. "It's the best comb in the world. It will make your pretty hair shine like a raven's wing."

Snow White could not resist this. She took the comb from the old lady and began to run it through her hair. Suddenly she fell to the floor.

The old woman laughed joyfully and hurried back to the castle to consult her mirror.

In the meantime the dwarfs returned home from work to find Snow White lying on the floor. They immediately suspected the wicked Queen of hurting her, and hurriedly removed the poisoned comb from her hair. When they had done this Snow White opened her eyes. The dwarfs made her promise never to open the door or the window to anyone again.

In the castle, the Queen was once more making evil plans, for the mirror had told her that Snow White was still alive. This time she decided to disguise herself as a farmer's wife, taking apples to market. Of course the best apple of all was full of poison.

The wicked Queen set out for the cottage of the seven dwarfs. At the door she stopped and knocked. "Who is it?" asked Snow White from the other side of the door. "I am a farmer's wife," said the Queen. "I was on my way to the market, but missed the path through the wood. I wonder if you could show me the way?"

Snow White peered out of the window. The farmer's wife looked so jolly and rosy-cheeked, and her apples shone red and green in their basket. "Surely this pleasant woman could not mean me any harm," thought Snow White. With this thought she put out of her mind all that the dwarfs had told her, and she opened the door. "Of course I will show you the way."

While Snow White was giving directions to the farmer's wife, the woman took a rosy, delicious-looking apple out of her basket and offered it to her. "Thank you for helping me," she said with a smile. "Enjoy this apple with my thanks."

Snow White took the apple and, waving goodbye to the farmer's wife, went into the cottage and shut the door. The apple was fragrant and it made her feel quite hungry. She could not resist taking a big bite.

No sooner had she done so than she fell down in a faint. The piece of apple lodged in her throat.

On their return from work the dwarfs discovered Snow White and quickly realised that her heart was no longer beating. Tearfully they sat down and thought about what they should do next, and after a while they decided to make a casket of the finest crystal. In this they would lay the body of Snow White on crimson cushions of the softest velvet. The casket would rest in her favourite leafy glade in the forest, watched over by her dearest friends.

Each day two dwarfs stood guard over the casket in which Snow White lay, looking more beautiful than ever. It is not surprising that a prince journeying through the forest felt that he must stop and admire her.

The dwarfs told him the sad story, and as they spoke the Prince raised the lid of the casket. He could not believe that Snow White was no longer alive, she was so beautiful. This sudden movement of the lid released the apple from Snow White's throat, and she sat up and blinked.

"Where am I?" she enquired. "Have I been asleep?"

The dwarfs crowded round, jumping for joy and laughing. Snow White caught sight of the Prince and a blush spread over her lovely cheeks. She smiled shyly.

The Prince helped Snow White out of the casket and lifted her onto his horse. "I shall take the Princess Snow White back with me to my father's palace," he told the dwarfs. "There she will always be safe from her wicked stepmother."

Though the dwarfs sadly bade their dear Snow White farewell, they knew that now she would be free from harm.

You can probably guess the end of this story. Snow White and the Prince fell in love and were soon married. The dwarfs were invited to the wedding and they gave Snow White a present of precious stones and gold which they had mined themselves.

As for the wicked Queen, she looked into her mirror just once more. What it told her so enraged her that she smashed it into a thousand fragments. Then she packed her belongings and set off for her own country, far beyond the mountains. If she ever got there no-one knows, for she was never seen again.

SINBAD THE SAILOR

The luckiest children in the whole of Baghdad were the grandchildren of Sinbad the Merchant. It was well known that he was the greatest story-teller in the city. In the evenings the children would sit enthralled as he told them of the great adventures he had experienced as a young man.

In his youth Sinbad had been a sailor. He owned ships in which he carried his merchandise over the Seven Seas to far-away lands. Many strange and wonderful sights had met his eyes and many exciting things had happened to him.

Sinbad's daughter often complained that it was almost impossible to get the children to bed, so spell-bound were they by their grand-father's tales.

If the children were asked which of the seven voyages of Sinbad they found the most interesting they would find it very difficult to choose one.

One might say that the time when their grandfather had mistaken a giant whale for an island and disembarked onto it from his ship was the best story of all. The whale had carried him away on its back and Sinbad would have surely drowned had not the whale cast him onto a small island.

This island was the one on which Sinbad had found the silver horse which belonged to King Mihrjan, who had later helped Sinbad to return to Baghdad on the very same ship on which he had set sail months before.

Then there was the adventure of the Island of Giants. Here Sinbad nearly lost his life.

The island was inhabited by terrible giants and dwarfs, who were extremely ugly and wicked. The sailors were all terrified of them.

The dwarfs captured Sinbad's ship, but he and some friends managed to escape and find their way to a huge palace with gates of blackest ebony.

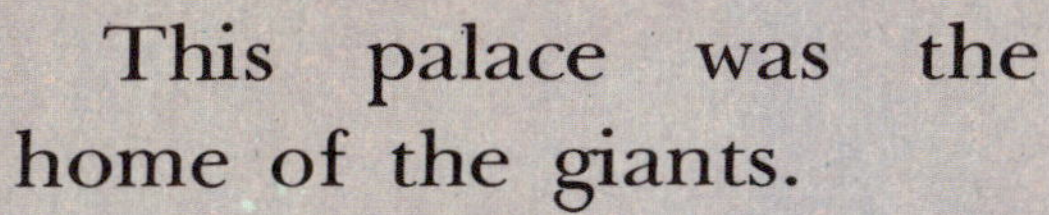

This palace was the home of the giants.

The biggest giant captured Sinbad and his companions and began to fatten them up but Sinbad refused to eat anything.

In due course, one by one, his companions were devoured by the giant. But the thin Sinbad and one of his friends escaped.

This was by no means the end of that story, for they had escaped from one danger into another just as horrifying.

Sinbad and his friend wandered into a part of the country inhabited by an enormous serpent. They climbed a tall tree to escape this monster but Sinbad's friend was soon claimed by it.

Sinbad spent an uncomfortable night but by morning the serpent had gone and Sinbad climbed down.

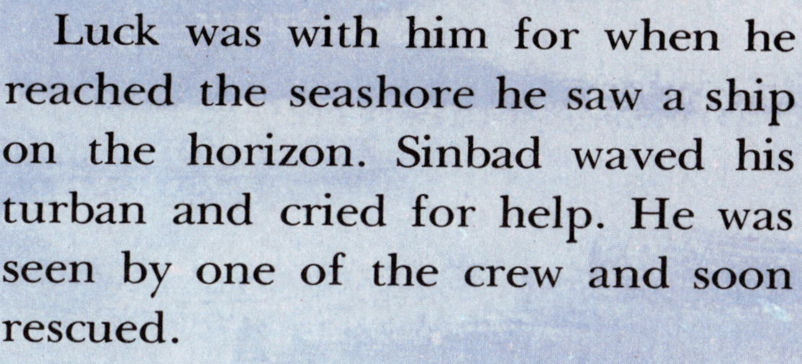

Luck was with him for when he reached the seashore he saw a ship on the horizon. Sinbad waved his turban and cried for help. He was seen by one of the crew and soon rescued.

The captain gave Sinbad one of his own suits to replace the rags which the poor merchant wore. He also told Sinbad that he could earn some money for himself by trading the goods of a passenger who had been lost on the voyage. Imagine the surprise of both Sinbad and the captain when upon unloading the goods it was discovered that they belonged to none other than Sinbad himself.

Thus Sinbad, despite his ordeals, returned home as wealthy as when he had left.

Another adventure that Sinbad described to his grandchildren was the one in which he visited an island inhabited by cannibals. In this story all Sinbad's friends reached an untimely end and he alone escaped to a place where he was welcomed by all the people and became a friend of the King himself.

In this land the people rode their horses bareback. Sinbad became wealthy by making bridles and saddles for the horses. Neither of these things had ever been seen in that land before and soon became very popular.

After some time, the King arranged a marriage for Sinbad to one of the ladies at the court.

It was not until his wife became very ill that Sinbad learned of a terrible custom of that country. If a wife died, her poor husband was not allowed to live, but was buried with her.

Sinbad, afraid that his wife might die, was once more forced to escape. He eventually found a ship upon which he embarked. This ship travelled to many places and Sinbad soon became wealthy and returned home.

A favourite story was that of the Old Man of the Sea, which the children turned into a game.

The strongest boy, Tariq, took the part of Sinbad and the others took turns being the Old Man of the Sea. This way they all got a ride on Tariq's back, for the Old Man of the Sea was known to climb onto men's backs and force them to carry him around until they died of exhaustion.

Sinbad had carried the Old Man for several days. One day he filled an empty gourd with juice from many grapes. This he left in the sun for a while. Then he offered the drink to the Old Man. The grape juice was strong and made the Old Man drowsy. He slipped and fell, hitting his head on a sharp stone. He lay without moving and Sinbad seeing that he was dead hurried away.

On his way to the seashore Sinbad encountered some people behaving very strangely. They were throwing lumps of clay at a multitude of monkeys high in a group of palm trees. Their action was made clear when Sinbad saw the angry monkeys retaliate by throwing coconuts at the people below. These coconuts were soon gathered into bags to be sold at the market.

Sinbad collected enough to pay a ship's captain for his passage back home.

The adventure Sinbad most often spoke about was when the Caliph sent him back to King Mihrjan with an important letter. Sinbad's ship was attacked by pirates and Sinbad and the crew were captured and sold into slavery.

Sinbad was bought by a wealthy ivory merchant. His job was to shoot as many elephants as he could, for the tusks were very valuable. Sinbad would climb a tree and aim his bow and arrows as the elephants passed beneath.

One day an elephant, bigger than he had ever seen, uprooted the tree upon which he sat and carried him away. He was taken to the Hill of the Elephants, where old elephants went to die. Here among the bones were many tusks. With these Sinbad bought his freedom and returned home even wealthier than before.

Each of these stories impressed Sinbad's grand-children and they never tired of hearing them. They told the stories to their own children, when they were grown, and they in turn were as enchanted by them as their parents had been.

Strangely enough, the story that was most often told was the one Sinbad had least liked to tell. The family all knew that he remembered it well, for he would pick up a large, shimmering diamond from a shelf and he would look a little afraid as he held it in his hand. It was all that remained from the most frightening adventure of all.

During his second voyage the ship Sinbad was embarked upon touched on an island which looked like paradise. Fruit and flowers grew in abundance.

The crew and passengers wandered about sampling the fruit, and Sinbad, who was tired, decided to rest in the sun under a shady tree. He must have slept for some considerable time for when he awoke the stars shone in the night sky and the ship was gone. Sinbad was alone and stranded. There was nothing for it, at daybreak he would have to begin searching for a way off the island. He passed a troubled night and in the morning set off to look for some sign of human habitation.

After walking for some time he came upon an extraordinary object. It was huge, white, and smooth. Before Sinbad had time to examine it, the sky was filled with the beating of mighty wings. A great shadow fell upon Sinbad and looking up he beheld a terrifying sight. It was the largest bird that he had ever seen. Sinbad had

heard tales of these giant birds. He knew that this must be a Roc and that the great white object nearby was its egg.

As the bird alighted Sinbad had an idea. He unwound his turban and attached one end of it to one of the Roc's legs, which was almost as wide as the trunk of a palm tree. Clinging very tightly to the other end, Sinbad waited for the giant bird to fly off and carry him with it.

At last the bird took to the air. They flew a great distance and finally landed on a high crag. Here Sinbad untied his turban and scuttled out of the bird's sight.

After a while he emerged from his hiding place and surveyed his surroundings.

On the ground great diamonds were strewn and among them Sinbad could see huge serpents slithering about. Sinbad knew that he must seek shelter from these serpents, which would surely become more lively as evening approached.

He climbed back onto the rock on which the giant bird had alighted. He now knew where he was. This was the fabled Valley of Diamonds, from which no man had ever emerged alive.

Sinbad was beginning to feel that all was lost when something hit him on the head. It was a piece of fresh meat. Sinbad remembered that he had been told of merchants who gathered diamonds from this terrible valley.

Fresh meat was thrown over the rocks into the valley in the hope that some of it would stick to the diamonds, as it was known that giant eagles picked up the meat and carried it to their nests. The merchants then collected the diamonds from the nests and sold them for vast sums of money.

Here was a way for Sinbad to escape. He filled his pockets with the biggest diamonds that he could find and then went in search of a large piece of meat. He soon found a piece almost as big as himself. He wrapped it round his body and secured it with his ever-useful turban. Then he lay quietly and waited.

Before long he heard the beating of powerful wings and found himself being once more lifted into the air. The flight was short and he was soon dropped into what turned out to be a huge nest.

The eagle began to peck at the meat in which Sinbad was wrapped, but before it could make a meal of him it was frightened off by loud shouting. Sinbad looked to see what was happening.

Men armed with clubs were scrambling over the edge of the nest. They were amazed to find Sinbad in it. When they heard his story they were even more surprised. He was the only man to have come out of the Valley of Diamonds.

Sinbad had no difficulty at all in selling the fabulous diamonds. One of them he kept as a reminder of his adventure.

When as an old man he sat with the fiery stone in his hand, he would sometimes start, as if he had been disturbed by the sound of mighty wings. Then he would shiver slightly and say to the children, "Enough stories for today, it's time you were all in bed."

RUMPELSTILTSKIN

A great many years ago there lived a miller. He was the owner of a rather dilapidated windmill and the father of a very beautiful daughter. The windmill, despite its age, was in good working order, and the miller managed to provide sufficiently for himself and his daughter with the money he received from grinding the wheat of his neighbours.

The miller's daughter Bella was quite content to allow her father to do the work. She spent most of her time sitting and watching him without lifting a finger to help. Despite her laziness, the miller was excessively proud of his daughter.

To hear him talk, one would think that her face resembled the bloom of a summer rose. Her hair was reported to be finer than spun silk, and as for her voice, it was so musical that, beside her, a nightingale would need to hide in shame at the poor quality of its singing. Not only did the miller boast about her beauty, but he also had a great deal to say about her many talents. In fact anything she turned her hand to was done many times better than anyone had ever done it before.

The boastful miller really believed all these things about Bella, and she too was almost convinced that they were true.

Anyone who came to the mill was subjected to endless tales about the wonderful daughter of the miller. No one dared to laugh or joke about what was said, for the miller was known for his short temper and strong fists.

One day it chanced that the King of that country was out riding with several of his courtiers. While riding they happened to pass the old mill. Bella was sitting on the doorstep brushing her hair. The King thought that never had he seen a young girl as lovely as this.

Dismounting, he led his courtiers towards the mill.

The miller, who had been looking out of the window, saw him and took him for a rich merchant or a wealthy lord. Here at last was someone who would appreciate his wonderful daughter. He hurried down the stairs to welcome his guests and invite them to partake of refreshment.

The King and his party were tired and thirsty after their long ride and were happy to accept the miller's hospitality. Bella was sent to fetch food and a jug of ale. The miller was pleased to observe the travellers following his daughter with their eyes.

As soon as she was out of the room he commenced boasting. The visitors had to hear all about her beauty and her many talents. The miller became more and more excited as he spoke: "...And best of all," he concluded, "you will never believe this, but my Bella can spin ordinary flax into thread of the purest gold."

Flax into gold! No one had ever heard of such a thing being done. The King found it very difficult to believe. He began to think how wealthy he could be if he had a wife who could perform such a marvellous feat. He decided on the spot to marry the girl and take her straight back with him to his palace.

The miller was astounded when the King revealed his identity. It was too wonderful that his daughter was to be a real queen. Bella was summoned to hear the good news. She herself found it very difficult to believe that all this was not a dream.

The king rose to take his leave having left instructions with the girl's father about the wedding.

Bella was taken to the palace without further ado, as the King wanted to know as soon as possible how she was able to turn flax into gold.

The same afternoon Bella was escorted by the Lord Chamberlain to a small turret room where a spinning wheel and a pile of flax had been prepared for her.

The Chamberlain left the poor girl in the locked room with the King's words ringing in her ears: "If by morning you have not succeeded in spinning this flax into gold, you will incur my greatest displeasure."

As Bella looked at the flax in dismay she wondered what her punishment for displeasing the King would be. There was no way to escape from the room and neither was there a way in which the flax could become gold. Bella sat down and sobbed.

Suddenly she jumped up in amazement as she felt a tap on her shoulder. In front of her stood the smallest man that she had ever seen. His clothes were extremely smart and he sported a fine moustache and a short ginger beard. "Ho, ho," he laughed, and his eyes twinkled, "I surprised you, didn't I?"

Bella looked at him timorously and stepped back a little. "You needn't be afraid," he continued. "I have come to help you. I am a man of great power. I am willing to put it at your disposal, but you must give me something in return. I think I would like the silver ring from your finger."

"Can you really help me?" begged the girl. "I must spin this flax into gold before morning and I do not even know how to start."

"No sooner said than done," said the little man. "Blink your eyes and look again." Bella did as he instructed. When she opened her eyes the little man was seated at the spinning wheel and in front of him a pile of gold thread was getting bigger and bigger as he spun. In no time at all the job was done. Before Bella could thank him both the little man and the ring from her finger were gone.

Bella heard a key being turned in the lock on her door. It opened to admit the King. He looked about him in disbelief at the strands of gold thread which lay all over the floor. "That old fool of a miller must have been speaking the truth after all," thought the King. "If she could do it once, she can do it again." His greedy eyes surveyed the gleaming thread. It would look fine made into bolts of cloth of gold to keep in his secret treasure chamber.

"Your work has pleased me," he said to the girl. "The thread which you have spun is of good quality, but I think that if the flax were better, the thread could be even richer. I wish you to spin some more. This time the flax will come from my own fields. I expect it to be ready by morning."

Bella was taken to a room which was strewn with flax which looked exactly the same as the flax which the little man had spun for her the night before. She was left alone to begin her work. Of course all she did was to sit and cry. It was not long before the little man once more made an appearance. This time he demanded the girl's locket and chain in return for spinning the flax into gold. She readily offered it to him and, as before, in no time at all the job was done.

Soon after the little man disappeared the King came to see if the flax had become gold. He praised Bella for her work and told her that if she spent just one more night spinning, then he would marry her with no further delay.

Bella had no choice but to follow the King into a third room where an even greater amount of flax had been left for her to spin. The poor girl knew that if the little man offered to help her again, she would have to send him away, for she had nothing to offer him in payment. As she was thinking about him the little fellow appeared.

"I know that you cannot reward me," he said, "but I shall still help you. Soon you will be a queen, and if one day you should chance to become a mother I shall take your first-born child in payment."

Bella was ready to agree to anything. She promised her first child to the little man. Soon her flax had been spun into gold and he was gone.

This time the King kept his word. Not long after, he and Bella were married, and a completely new way of life began for the miller's daughter. She had fine clothes and servants to command. Never did she have to lift a finger to do work of any kind. She was as happy as could be. After a year of marriage she became the mother of a beautiful baby girl. The King called his daughter Adorabella, and she was soon loved by all.

One morning, as the Queen sat with her daughter on her knee, she heard a little voice which sounded vaguely familiar. "I have come for my payment," it said. She looked around. Sitting on the windowsill was the little man that she had forgotten all about. Surely he could not mean to take the Princess Adorabella!

The Queen held the child closer to her. "Please, do not take my baby," she begged. "I will give you money, or jewels, or anything you wish, if only you will spare my child."

The little man looked at the baby. He thought of how he would take her home with him, where she would grow up to be his servant. He thought that he would play a joke on the Queen first.

"I will spare your daughter," he lied, "if you can guess my name. You will have three chances. If you are unable to guess correctly, the child will be forfeit."

The Queen eagerly consented to this and began to think of names to suit the little man. "Is your name Gingerbeard? Is it Twinkle-eye? Or perhaps it is Thumbkin?" she asked.

To each question her tiny visitor replied with a laugh and a shake of the head. "You have two more chances," he said finally and, with a little jump, disappeared.

The poor Queen spent the next few days trying to think up different names. She announced a competition to her servants for the most unusual name. None of this helped very much, for the next time that the little man appeared she was unable to give him the right answer. Now she was almost in despair.

One of the royal huntsmen heard two servants talking about the Queen's competition. They were trying to think up the funniest names they had ever heard.

"I know a very unusual name," thought the huntsman to himself. "I will tell the Queen about the funny little man I saw when I was in the forest."

He hurried to the royal chambers, where he was received immediately by the Queen herself, who by now was almost out of her mind with worry.

The huntsman bowed low and began to speak: "Your Majesty, when I heard about your competition I decided to come at once. I have a very good name for you. I will tell you how I came to hear of it.

"Last week, while I was walking through the forest following the tracks of a deer, I thought I heard a voice singing and I tried to see where it was coming from.

"All of a sudden I saw a small clearing. In the centre was a small fire. Dancing round it, and singing gleefully to himself, was the oddest little person I have ever seen. His clothes were brightly coloured, and he had a little pointed beard. He did not see me, but I shall never forget him.

"I think I can remember the words he was singing. They sounded something like this." At this point the huntsman cleared his throat and began to sing in a funny croaking voice:

"Dance and sing and jump for glee,
No one knows my name but me.
Little recks my Royal Dame
Rumpelstiltskin is my name!"

As the huntsman performed the song, the Queen wrote down the words. Now she knew that she would be able to outwit the cocky little man.

Several days later he made what he said was his final appearance. The Queen tried some of the names which her servants had suggested to her. After shaking his head to each one, her unwelcome visitor danced nearer and nearer to the baby. Finally he tried to snatch the Princess from her cot. "Now she is mine!" he shouted in triumph, which soon turned to rage as the Queen said: "Wait! Is your name Rumpelstiltskin?"

The little man shouted and stamped his feet as he slowly became red and then purple in the face. Then, with a great howl of rage, he quite disappeared, never to be seen again.

No one could have been happier than the Queen when Rumpelstiltskin disappeared. At last her baby was safe. She rewarded the huntsman handsomely for his help, and made him promise never to speak of the matter again.

The King never found out about the Queen's dealings with Rumpelstiltskin, but he often wondered at her great dislike for his fine cloth-of-gold cloak. Had she not spun the thread herself out of ordinary flax?

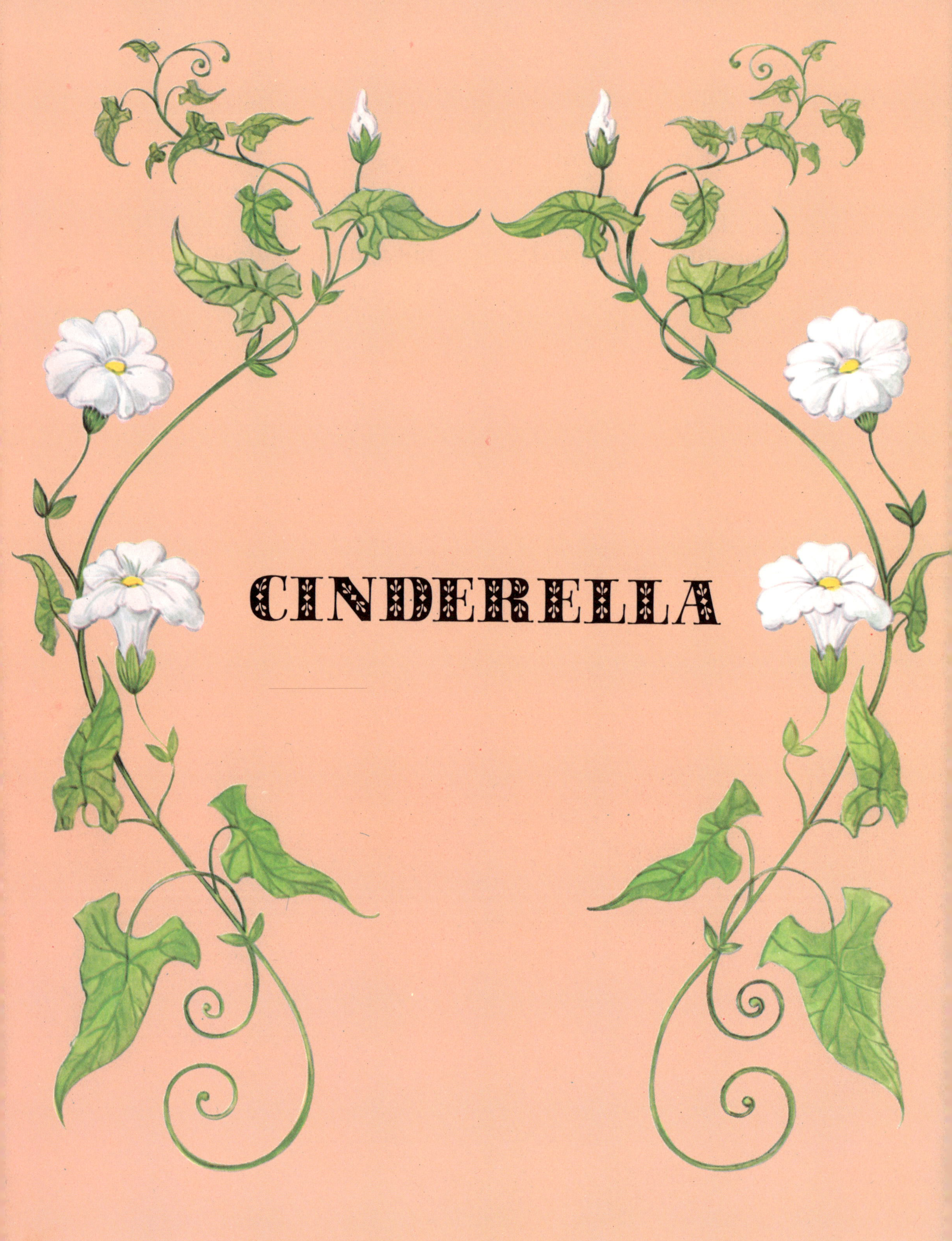

CINDERELLA

LONG ago, in a faraway land, there lived a rich merchant whose wife died, leaving him with a small daughter called Ella.

After some years the man had remarried. His second wife was very proud and cruel, and loved no one except her own two daughters.

All three of them were mean and spiteful. They bullied and ill-treated poor Ella. She was made to work hard and her clothes soon became tattered and dusty with the ashes from the fire, so they found a new name for her—Cinderella.

Cinderella's two stepsisters were as ugly as they were spiteful and forced her to become their servant. She had to scrub floors and wash dishes, and get up before dawn each day to clean out the cinders in the hearth.

Despite their fine clothes and jewels they could not hide their coarse features, and were very jealous of Cinderella, who though poorly dressed and dirty, still remained far prettier than they.

They constantly made fun of her, and tried to upset her. They even tore up her invitation to Prince Charming's ball, the very ball at which he was going to choose a wife.

They stood in their finery sneering at the poor girl. "You should never have been invited in the first place," said the elder. "A scrawny, dirty girl like you would never dare show her face at the ball." Cinderella cried bitterly when her sisters left for the ball. She had so much wanted to go.

Suddenly a bright light appeared in the corner of the room. Cinderella looked up in amazement. There stood a strangely dressed lady, in a tall hat and with a wand.

"I am your fairy godmother," she said. "Bring me a pumpkin, four mice and a rat, and you shall go to the ball."

The surprised girl did as she was told. With a wave of her wand the fairy godmother transformed the pumpkin into a magnificent coach with a coachman, drawn by four splendid horses.

Then she waved her magic wand once more and lo! Cinderella herself was dressed in the most beautiful gown she had ever seen. On her feet were slippers of sparkling glass.

"Enjoy yourself at the ball, my dear, but be sure to return before midnight," said the fairy godmother with a final wave of her wand.

When Cinderella arrived at the ball, she looked so beautiful, that the Prince led her into the ballroom. Everyone wondered who the lovely young girl could be. “Perhaps she is a very rich princess from a faraway land . . . ,” they whispered.

Cinderella looked so different, that her two ugly sisters did not recognise her. They were too busy grumbling that the Prince danced only with her.

Suddenly Cinderella remembered the words of her fairy godmother. It was nearly midnight, she must hurry away before something dreadful happened. She left the Prince in mid-dance, and ran out of the ballroom as fast as she could.

Hurrying down the marble steps of the palace Cinderella heard the clock beginning to chime. Midnight had arrived. In her dismay, she tripped and lost one of her pretty glass slippers.

As soon as she reached home the beautiful golden coach, the horses and the coachman disappeared, as did her magnificent ball gown.

She stood once more in her kitchen, dressed in the tattered rags she had worn before.

Prince Charming picked up the tiny glass slipper which Cinderella had lost on the palace stairs.

The next morning servants were summoned to carry it on a cushion of velvet through the streets of the towns and villages, so that all the young girls in the land would have a chance to try it on.

The Prince promised to wed the one on whom the slipper was a perfect fit.

He had been trying to match the slipper for several days, but had not been able to do so.

At the house of the ugly sisters both tried to squeeze their huge feet into the tiny glass slipper. Of course they were quite unable to do so.

They sniggered to themselves when the Prince's servant asked Cinderella if she would like to try on the slipper.

"That stupid girl does not stand a chance," they said.

Cinderella immediately recognised the slipper as the one she had lost after the ball. She knew that it would fit.

Despite the protests of the ugly stepsisters, the servant kneeled down and slipped it on her foot. The tiny glass slipper fitted perfectly.

As soon as Cinderella put on the slipper, the other one appeared as if by magic, and then the beautiful dress which she had worn to the ball. Of course it was the fairy godmother who made it all happen.

The Prince was overjoyed to find Cinderella again and soon asked her to become his wife.

As for the ugly stepsisters and their cruel mother, from that day on they had to do their own cleaning and cooking.

Princess Cinderella, happily married to her Prince Charming, would never have to do such work again.